Florp Merlorp

I am a cartoon man

James Zintel

jameszin.tel

ISBN-13: 978-0-9950059-1-4

Florp Merlorp: I Am a Cartoon Man by James Zintel, First Printing, 2019. Published by HyperWrench Productions.
No portion of this publication may be used or reproduced in any manner whatsoever without the written permission
of the author, except in the case of select quotations or reprints in the context of reviews.

Slight of hand

Is this Dillbert?

Terrifying tales

Died on world 1-1

Gotta charge 'em all

Potions class dropout

A good friend to have

Humanity's best defence.

A terrible mistake.

Sensible bites always

Riding space mountain.

Dangerous attitude room.

Fine dining

Six sided die

From the top of the key

Unleash the beast

Don't do this

Stop. Hammer time.

The art of seduction

A clean energy

Teenage mutant ninja traitor

Whallopin' websnappers

Amen.

Same ass time

And the cats and the cradle

Doin' the humpty hump

More like cruel ranch

L'il Scribbl

Still better than emus

Pokin' cows, breaking hearts

Are there still Quiznos?

Splashy Sword Smackdown!

Scottish accents for all!

Doin' the humpty hump

Playa two

WE ALL LAUGHED WHEN A CHICKEN WAS ELECTED PRESIDENT.

WE GIGGLED WHEN PRESIDENT CLUCKBUCK SIGNED THE EXECUTIVE ORDER TO BUILD A BRIDGE OUT OF CORN.

THEN THE DISSADENTS STARTED TO GO MISSING...

NEWSLY TIMES

ANOTHER PESIDENTIAL CRITIC GONE MISSING

THIRD IN AS MANY DAYS

Buck, buck, doom

The 'S' stands for shope

The price of business

Honey baked hardon

Sorry.

DANG!
AMAZON TREATS IT'S WAREHOUSE EMPLOYEES TERRIBLY.

OOOH!
FIRE TABLETS ARE ON SALE.
I'LL GET TEN.

Fit for the pit.

One tree enters, one cat leaves

Mark comes marching one by one

Feliz Navidad!

IF YOU INVENT SOMETHING
THAT'S IDIOT PROOF, THE
WORLD WILL INVENT A
BETTER IDIOT.

MEET JUSTIN.

I PUT NICKELS
IN MY TRAIL MIX!

HE'S THE BEST
IDIOT THE WORLD
HAS MADE.
AND HE'S YOUR
SISTER'S NEW BOYFRIEND.
AND HE'S COMING TO
CHRISTMAS DINNER.

Happy Holidays

Like Wayne Gretzky!

No dinky Tinker Toy

Auld Lang Syne!

Occupied!

New Year's Slay

Crack is whack!

Burney the Alpaca

Country roads

Once-ler in a life time

The Haunter of Hill House

Safe word for initative

A respectful OH YEAH!

A genocide of a deal

Harasssssssssssment

Altering the deal.

THE EARTH, IS HOME TO 7.5 BILLION PEOPLE

BILLIONS LIVING THEIR LIVES

GOING TO WORK,

EATING A MEAL

HUGGING A LOVED ONE.

AND AT LEAST ONE PERSON WHO IS WEIRDLY ENRAGED BY FUNKO POPS.

I DON'T GET THE APPEAL!

And ya don't stop

Pee pee roni

Answer the collect call

Three star man.

Nanna Nanna

Modern romance.

To the window

AND IF YOU THREW A PARTY
AND INVITED EVERYONE YOU KNEW

WELL YOU WOULD SEE, THE BIGGEST
GIFT WOULD BE FROM ME

AND THE CARD ATTACHED
WOULD SAY

IMMA
CUT
YOU!

Solid gold

Two thousand one nine

Booobies

It's a mean cold

Clam yourself

....until now

Cowardly lot

Pitching in

Tony Denza

Bleached is the new orange

Mon amie

Not a fink

Dream-squacher

Day Job Steve Austin

We didn't start the fire

Right handy of doom

Saskatoon Banksy

Hoppy Easter

Daly bread

This the day of our wedding.

Sharing it with loved ones and well wishers.

And that one guy who thought it was okay to wear a baseball cap.

THE INVITE SAID BUSINESS CASUAL.

PUSH

The mullet of headwear

SITTING HERE AWASH IN THOUGHT.

CONTEMPLATING THE EVENTS THAT LEAD ME TO THIS POINT.

WHY DO HOTELS INSIST WE WATCH OURSELVES POOP?

Through the looking glass

Figuratively cool, it's actually quite warm

Best offense

Best in life

Lebronto Park

Gildan Matchmaker

Humpty Bumpty

Beat goes on.

Ghost Milk

Bearly beloved

Awkward is what you make it

Anime hump day

Emmet Otter Juglas Band

The hand that feeds